Cover photo by Arthur French
Ipplepen, Devon 1994
Design by Dave Percival

Terce drawing by Arthur French

Kalendar illustration by Stainedglassinc.com

Back cover photo
Passport portrait, 2 August 1962

This edition 2024
Second reprint
ISBN: 978 1 7385743 1 5

Proceeds to be donated to Afrinspire,
a favourite charity of Joy & Arthur French

tretheweypress@gmail.com

TRETHEWEY PRESS

COLLECTED POETRY

BY

JOY FRENCH

First published
by Trethewey Press
1994 - 1998

NOTES & QUERIES (1994)

ISBN 0 09528720 1 3

SECOND THOUGHTS (1996)

ISBN 0 9528720 0 5

TERCE (1998)

ISBN 0 9528720 2 1

(The section entitled 'Kalendar' was also published as a small booklet)

COMING FORTH

Poems Previously Unpublished

INTRODUCTION

In memory of my dear mother Joy (1921-2007).

Her three self-published poetry volumes, originally available via Amazon, are generally unavailable nowadays. I felt it would be a fitting way to mark the 30th anniversary in 2024 of her first book, “Notes & Queries”, by collating all three collections into a single compilation for all to enjoy.

I rarely wrote any poetry myself; my mother was definitely the main talent in that regard in our family (although I recall my brother Patrick won a poetry award at university). The main time I had any poetic inspiration myself was after Joy’s funeral in June 2007. A few lines poured out of me, unplanned, unexpected and fully formed, about that life-changing experience. I didn’t claim it to be anything like the quality of her standard, but I sensed a certain similarity in style – as if the wordsmith was sending me a final message.

For me, these volumes of her verses capture and summarise my impression of her life in Devon during the 1990s, the first decade she and my father Arthur spent there after retirement to the West country. I treasure the original copies which she signed for me, and hope this new collection reaches and inspires others.

Dan French
tretheweypress@gmail.com

When I read these poems again I am struck by Joy's lifelong faith, her endurance, her wit, and the breadth of her reference. She often borrows from other people's poetry – such as Eliot, one of her favourites – as well as the many references to Christian themes. And every time it fits perfectly in her own work; it's as if she brings new life to it.

The love of poetry is one thing I have inherited from her, which I am extremely glad of. I have written poems, songs and what I call ditties all my life – not many published yet, but watch this space! I studied the great poets of the past when I was at university, and Joy's recurrent iambic rhythm, like a heartbeat, echoes and resonates with much that I learnt to love there.

Another thing I admire very much about Joy's poetry is the way she develops an idea so concisely into a reflection, often on her own life, or on life in general, with the minimum of words and allusions. There's truth in the words, and truth is always complex; and yet, a poem can convey it with a few words, a hint or two will do it, in between the words. Thanks for the inspiration.

Patrick French

CONTENTS

"Farmer's Funeral" has appeared in "The Countryman"

"Element of Love" was read at the wedding of Dan French & Ruth Hammond, 1998

"Litany for St. Luke" first appeared in "Second Thoughts"

NOTES & QUERIES

Paradise Lost

There was an apple.
I saw it; I knew it.
So perfect my knowing
I held it within me
In whole completion:
Eating it,
Bite by bite,
An after-act,
A sacrament.

But oh!
The phone rang, and I went
Half-apple in hand,
And set it down
Somewhere, somewhere,
On the way.

Now through my world I go wandering,
Stumbling, blundering,
A hole within me,
Seeking a lost completion.

When shall I be made whole?

Prayer (when not feeling much like it)

O Lord, a lump
I come to you;
Heavy and dull
I hold to you;
Stuck in the mud
I cling to you;
Half asleep
I turn to you;
Left for dead
I look for you.

I can do nothing for myself
But you can:
Send, if you will, a time of refreshing
Even to clay.

Jacob's Ladder

Your small green steps
Reaching to heaven
I found first
On a Sussex heath,
And thought a rarity.
Here, in the West,
You scramble about my garden,
Common as weeds.

Yet Jacob's dream
Retains its ancient power:
The angels still ascend
And return; bearing what gift
Not to be hoarded,
Nor wasted?

Padstow

The boats sleep in the harbour,
Obedient as sheep,
Journeys over, facing one way,
At rest; and I read the names:
Alethea, Daisy, Millicent,
Susie, and Ellen May.

And up the steep hill
Beneath the granite church
Invisible among its trees
Save for a golden clock-face
Remarking Time,
The gravestones sleep in the churchyard,
Obedient as sheep
Waiting the shepherd;
And I read the names again:
Alethea, Daisy, Millicent,
Susie, and Ellen May.

Dreaming of what journeys past,
What unimaginable Way to come?

The Way

Here on the tightrope I –
measuring quick and slow,
balancing joy and grief
– imperfectly go.

The Fall repeated each day
is daily, hourly, forgiven;
savouring bruise and balm
I know Sin shriven.

How should I do but bless
on high, or low?
The paradox is grace:
I stumble, yet go.

Scrutinies

As a child
I feared most
Sharp eyes of
Playground children
Perceiving my
Infirmity.

Grown now
Yet I fear
Wounded eyes
Glimpsed in glass
Betraying sens-
-ibility.

Come the end
Shall I fear
His eyes
Who fashioned me
Outgazing my
Humility?

Rain In The Morning

The rain drops on the window pane
With small infrequent kisses;
Just so, light liking an affair
Simply of hit or miss is.

But you, my love, in such full flood
Transparency embrace
As makes perception clearer yet:
Your waters, and my glass.

Out Of Season

Old age
Is time to dwell in the country; youth
Time to live in towns.
For the young are incessantly seeking some
Inaccessible treasure hid
In metropolitan mines;
Whilst in age
Leaf-fall and spring-flood
Acquire a particular meaning
Unrecognised hitherto.

But where, oh heart, to spend my
Querulous middle-age,
This autumn of discontent?

God defend me in suburbia.

Walking At Night

Darkness my solace, into your embrace
Night for my comfort, wind in my face,
Darkness my solace, into you I pace.

Walking in the blackness the blacker flood,
Going uncertain, yet going good,
Walking in blackness I plunge my step.

Glory to darkness and things of night,
Refuge from brittle, from withering light!
Glory to silence and solitude: hark!
Surges my soul as I stride in the dark.

Deus Absconditus

Content? Hardly that.
Not for me the images
Of satisfaction, feeding full upon
Green pastures, sweet waters.

Rather, a willed acceptance
Of how You choose to be:
The mystery hidden
Since before Time was,
Compelling our perusal;
The irresolvable tension
Betwixt knowing and unknowing,
Balancing in the awareness
That what our search requires
Must be Your presence, somewhere.

So Pascal got it right:
Hunger implies the bread,
And our questioning, Your existence.

Migraine

The headache hasn't gone,
It pins me to the pillow;
I move my head to the right
And left, but it won't be shifted.
Better to stay still.

Forty years and more
Migraine has been my lot:
Vision dissolving in patches, and
The bright aurora.
I wear the pain like a hat,
But it won't be lifted.

Cost Of Living

I am God's tenant
In a tied cottage:
This body, hands and feet
And the heart that beats
Awake at night.

Summertime
Loving was easy;
Now, in autumn,
Cost of living
Ever-rising,
Should I complain if
He puts up the rent?

October

Even a breath of air
Loosens the chestnuts, and to ground they go,
Sun-shot with gold. Why against reason
Does grief clutch at the heart, as each bright frigate
Sets sail for nowhere?
Is it because
Here in the autumn of age, I see myself
In the helpless pilfered tree, and fear the fall?

Step closer; every empty twig
Is tipped with next year's sticky buds
You could not see for leaves.

Incarnation

In newborn features we behold
The father's brow, the mother's eyes,
No whit astonished to remark
Such mingling of properties.

In Jesus Christ, this child newborn,
We sense the God; we see the man.
Such mingling of properties
Alarms us more than angels can.

O Jesus Christ, O Child so wise,
Have pity on your silly sheep!
Open our eyes; open our hearts
That we may see, and love, and weep.

Retrospect

Every sentence spoken, I can see
The right way to have said it;
Every visit ended, I can tell
The right way to have behaved.

Thus we progress with backward-looking steps,
And, when we come to die, may perhaps discover
How we ought to have lived; but how to die?
What after death will teach us that?

Makerere

In the hilltop chapel
God is made and broken;
Africa astir without
The mighty words are spoken;
And meekly kneeling on our knees
We take His earthly token.

Thanks be to Thee, O God:
Praise be to Thee, O Christ.

SECOND THOUGHTS

For A.K.F. and P.B.
with love and thanks

PEOPLE

Farmer's Funeral

From all over they've come, from fifty miles,
Solid men, encased in Sunday black
Creased from the wardrobe, tight under the arms
And their massive wives, rosy and wrinkled in hats,
Hats appropriate, kept for such an occasion.
And when they sing, the thick westcountry voices
Resonate deep in the red walls of the church,
Deep in the flagstones, deep where the ancestors lie.
And all is as before, and will be again,
As the priest says the everlasting prayers,
And the farmers rumble "Amen".

Outside, in the shivering churchyard,
The talk is all of people.
"Where's Phil?" "Seen Tom?" "How's the boy?"
No word, out here, of the topic
Fuming in all their breasts:
The fate of cattle.
They'll keep that for the Church Hall
And the tea.

For G.J.T.

And I remember
Watching you walk down the High
Capped and gowned
Towards Schools,
One bright morning in wartime.
The stance alert,
Taut, reined-in
Like a horse before the race;
The head,
Learning's chalice,
Carefully borne
Erect,
So as not to spill
One
        precious
                        drop.

First Cousin Once Removed

She sits
Caged in her deafness
On the edge
Of the sofa,
Not certain who we are.
Her hair
(Once lovingly permed),
A white thatch,
Ragged; unfamiliar.
Convicts and the insane
Are cropped like this;
She is neither,
But can no longer manage
Routine of brush and comb.
She croaks
Disconnected comments.
Her stalwart husband
Feeds her with cake.
We bring strawberries
Which she consumes, untidily,
But with apparent pleasure:
Then makes gestures
To be taken to the toilet.
She will be 90 next month:
The prospect is uncertain.

In Memoriam H.D.

Hilda,
You would have made a good Abbess.
I can just see you
On that bleak northeastern shore
Cherishing and chivvying
Your young (male and female
Mixed, as in proper family)
And praying; always that.

Latterly
The sun called you south;
And the postcards arrived
In your upright, untidy hand,
From Montpellier: some ancient church,
Ruinous and holy,
Where the curé, recognising a saint,
Had offered you communion.

But chiefly I remember
That cherished garden,
Your voice, husky and eager,
As you gathered flowers;
Moving like a bee from flower to flower,
Topic to topic;
Whilst I stood, hands full of blossom,
Knowing, somehow, a blessing.

In that New Town wilderness
You were a spring, the water of life.
Now the spring sinks back into the earth,
But we – we have been refreshed.

Bosnia

Never before
Such mockery?

The creaking convoy
Pathetic, bathetic,
Old men, women, children
– So many children!
Faces carved
To icons of loss,
Lacking food
    Water
    Hope,
Lumbers into sight
On the TV screen.

And beside the road
Soldiers in battledress
Grinning, sneering,
Suddenly start
A mocking dance,
Waving green branches –
A May Day travesty?

Never before
Such cruelty?
First-century Palestine
Springs suddenly to mind.

SEASONS

February

Bitter, uncertain spring;
Gray skies, green haze,
An aching wind;
And the landscape cold, unaroused
By the yet invisible sun.

March

Now winter's bond is broken,
The sullen frozen sky
Is loosed in swooping clouds and dancing rain,
And freed my heart again.

Late Rose

The sky grew gray;
And then, as the rain began,
I watched a rose
Full-blown
Drop, drop, drop
Her petals, one by one,
With a silent flurry,
Down to the shivering grass.
So simple, so inevitable-seeming,
Why did my heart cry out
In sudden pain, to reverse it?

September

Now shattered is the azure dome of summer:
The equinoctial gales have cracked its surface.
Cloud upon cloud, the jagged fragments scatter,
Diffuse, disperse, in dwindling depth and distance.

The waste of summer dies in hearth and bonfire;
Consuming fire
Licks round the leaves, chuckles and coughs at ash-logs.
(Their burning done, the ashes yet are fertile.)

The year stands still; the earth renews her being;
The water falls, as falling is its nature;
Lilies embrown their frozen white perfection,
And dancing dragonflies have space until sundown.

All things in ripeness wait their due completion.
O heart of discontent! where is my harvest?

CHURCH-GOING

Litany for St. Luke

Sit by the fire time,
Darkening at tea time,
Letters to friends time,
Brooding with books time,
        Poems emerging.

Beeches ablaze time,
Fall of the leaf time,
Bonfire-y smell time,
Mushrooms to pick time;
        Poems ripe.

Prayer in a New York Apartment

Feast of the Epiphany

The crucifix stands
On the bedroom shelf,
Gathering dust, alone.

Created dust
Falls round the Uncreated.
What the city rejects
Here finds rest.

Crouched, thus, in discomfort,
The requiring mind enquires
Is it habit, self-consolation,
Or a fond attachment to past happiness
That brings me to my knees
On the yellow dusty floor,
While below, the garbage trucks
Grin like a dog and run about the city,
And the fire-engines' wail
Anticipates Gehenna?

I think it is not habit
(For habits can be changed) nor the desire
For comfort (what comfort do You offer,
You frozen on Your cross?)
And to revive the memories of summer
Renews the pain of loss.

It is the abrogated might of love
That thus compels me to your Calvary,
To celebrate, anew, Epiphany.

Christmas
(somewhat after Betjeman)

Some ways, indeed, are rather odd
We celebrate the birth of God.
We hoover all the obvious floors,
Stick bits of holly to our doors,
Stand Christmas cards on every shelf,
And grant a holiday to self.
Is this the way to greet you, Lord,
Year after year? I guess you're bored!

This time I really would do better,
And so begin this birthday letter.
O teach us to redeem the time,
And, as the bells of midnight chime,
Offer a gift more rare than nice,
Costly yet simple, without price,
The gift from which all blessings start,
A thankful and a contrite heart.

Feast of St Lucy,
December 13th 1995

Yes

Little in life we know;
Be not deceived.
It matters less the blow
Than how received.

Fight or flight: the options
We learn to use.
Which, in the midnight garden,
Did He choose?

Not fight, the way of Peter;
Nor flight (the rest of the band).
Voices and torches crowding,
He chose to stand.

He stood: the last temptation
Recoiled on Satan's head.
He stands, the chalice accepted;
He lives, who was dead.

BIRDS, BEASTS, and a FISH

Visitation

Heron
High in heaven
Riding rooftops
Resting on ridge
Slowly, sedately
Stepping on slates
Ferocious eye
Fixing fishpond;

Suddenly stretching
Widening wings
Darkening daylight
Exiting eastwards
Effortlessly
Wordlessly

You wonder!

Goosey Goosey

Those arrows!
Harold at Hastings
Hideously
Through the eye,
And Rufus the Red
Far in the Forest
Mysteriously!

Again, at Agincourt,
A whistle on the wind,
A scream from the sky!

Shakespeare's sonnets,
Pepys' prose –
Through what wild centuries
Roves back the goose?
And when did it stoop
To propaganda?

The Age Electronic
Passes me by.
I prefer a pen,
Being, in matters mechanic,
A proper goose.

Fish

For a line-drawing by Kenneth Annat

I
see all
assess all
utter
nothing

I enclose all
synthesise all
weaving the pattern of my own meanders
and utter
nothing

My shape is taut
My tail stiff
My lips shut
Expressing
nothing

You cannot hurt me, nor you, nor you
Who gape at me through the glass
With idiotic gaze;
But if you take me out of my element
I shall die.

Let me alone
In the asylum of my own creating
Silently circling
A round
E Y E.

Hit

He hit it!
But the rabbit raced on
Paws jerking in rhythm,
Whilst the body sprawled
White fur and golden blood
On the highway of death.

And the cars raced on,
He his way and we ours.
No stop to check
Or break a neck.
But the paws, the fur, the blood
Hit me.

Cat-a-strophe

My big fat Tigger
(One hundred and more, in cat years)
Insinuates himself
Through the kitchen flap
And processes down the path.

The wisp of a kitten
(Six weeks, if that)
Arches his spiny back,
Each hair erect;
Snarls like a tiger, and hisses
(Where did he learn the art?)
And, in excess of feeling,
Drops two small scraps
Of excrement
Beneath his own back paws.

His elder
Permits his nostrils
One delicate sniff;
Flicks his bellrope tail,
Pads ponderously by
– A feline QE2 –
On the other side.

APOLOGIA

Metanoia

I drank a bitter cup
And oh! the taste was bitter.

I endured a pain
So hard, it seemed, so long.

That halfway through
I hesitated, faltered, almost fainted.

Sloth said: Give o'er,
But someone else said No,
Go on until the end.
I did not know
The reason why, but knew it must be so.

And I went on.

All this I had in dream;
Now comes the living of it,
None other than by grace.

Ring of Words

Long ago
And far away
In another age
I found it,
And took it to use,
Being maiden
And finding it fit the finger.

Neglected often
Yet unforgotten
At a touch, a rub,
The genie stirs.
A fitful spirit,
Rather invoked
Than commanded,
Preferring the moment
Less propitious
When the phone rings,
The kettle boil,
Or the person from Porlock calls.

Distractions concluded
At length, at last,
In silence, in patience,
In self-abnegation
Animus meus
Resumes his task:
Inspiring dry bones
With breath of the spirit,
Linking their order
In lively abandon –
See, how it comes!

My part, now, to set down
This.

The Element of Love

Pebbles under water
Are fairer far
Than those you hold in your hand.
Do not take them up in your hand;
Let them lie in the water.

Seaweed in the rock-pool
Unfolds its fronded lace;
Bird in the wide air
Lives in its pinion's race;
You may pluck the weed or cage the bird
In an alien place;
You have lost the grace.

Love is your element
And in your face
I see reflected
Beauty and grace
Not yours, but lent
By love's own true intent
Through my embrace.

Do not fear that love may pass,
That in your looking-glass
Your radiant countenance
May dim to commonplace
Or lose its grace;

Love is my element
That am your counterpart,
And love in either heart
Sustains the other;

We, loving lovers,
Our element shall prove
More durable than air
Or salt sea water;
We will unfold, or fly,
Or bright as pebbles lie
In still content;

Love given and received
Is love well spent.

Nightmares

The images of death recede:
The shattered skull, the bloodied hands;
The hair grown white I glimpse as mine;
The sudden fog confronting me.

These are the terrors of the night
Which reasoning daytime would undo,
Resolve the themes, elucidate,
Say 'This is false, though that be true.'

Yet still that window opens wide,
The curtain flaps, the cold wind blows;
I lie upon the bed of rack
And screams like living things are torn
From some deep centre ……
Waking brings
No solace to such agony,
Only reluctant, scorching tears.

Awareness

Let us thoughtfully consider and give praise
To the works of the Lord our God.
A sky new-made each morning,
ever since mornings were thought of,
Beggars imagination;
Seventy different kinds of leaf, in my garden alone,
Are but the beginning of invention.
But the mind, the mind of God!
That knows me better than I know myself,
And has known – and will know –
each of his creatures forever!
The only ascription that is not presumption
Is holy awe, and silence.

ENDPIECE

The Third Day

(On seeing a "Gardeners' World" programme)

The Cycad, tree of Paradise,
Is too primeval to be nice.
Each Adam tree displays his rod,
Each Eve her bosom bares to God.
Such boldness causes no offence:
"'Tis Prelapsarian innocence!"

TERCE

Dedicated to
The Revd. Mother and Sisters O.S.B.
St Mary's Abbey, West Malling
with love and thanksgiving

INTROIT

Global Warning

Yes; they knew winter, the ancestors.
Keats observed the hare
Trembling in frozen grass;
Christina,
Swathed in the petticoats her age demanded,
Yet sensed the earth, iron-hard,
Touched water's stony face.
Nearer home
Laurie Lee felt the wind's teeth,
Saw the star's talons.

We, with our central heating,
Snuggle in Global Warming,
As the Earth cracks, melts, dissolves.

First Cousin, now Removed

How far you have journeyed!
You have gone so far
The world you inhabit
Is as foreign to us
As the world of the newborn.
Like them, you lie
Swaddled and padded,
Eyes not quite closed, nor open,
Fingers fretting feebly
For something? We cannot tell.

The voices surround me:
“Speak to her! Say your name!
Tell her who you are!
Perhaps she will understand.”

Such interference
With your important business –
The business of dying –
Would be impertinence.
I touch your fingers, your hand,
And mean Fare Well
Into wherever you are travelling,
Dear Cousin,
Now more than once removed.

News Item: Syria

One had thought the rack
Outmoded,
Along with Guy Fawkes,
His beard, and his pointed hat.

So it comes as a shock
To read of a man –
A poet, Faraj –
In a Syrian jail
Twisted and bent
By what is described as
“Hyperextension”.
(Yes; it takes one a moment
To comprehend fully
What that must mean.)

Imputing their sins
To others’ example
They name their invention
(Like Adam, like Eve,
In Paradise Garden)
“The German Chair”.

They deceive
Neither God nor Allah.

News Item: Algeria

"Shoot me!" begged the boy,
Preferring the brief bullet's thud
To the lingering slice of the knife.

But –
Like his father's
mother's
brothers' –
His throat
Was cut.

Prodigal's Brother

I am that elder brother,
Coming in at the end of the tale;
The taken-for-granted one, I trudge
Out to my work in the field each day,
Watching my father watch the road,
Eyes on the distance, the far horizon,
Oblivious of me.

Now I come back, sweaty and stiff with toil,
And I hear music, laughter! There
He stands, wearing the best robe,
Ring on his finger – but I can see
The ingrained dirt of him; I smell the swine.
They have killed the fatted calf? that calf was mine!
Or should have been, by rights. I watched his birth,
A little bull, the first-born; like myself.

First-born! a shroud of loss engulfs me;
*I go heavily** … and these fools are dancing!
She is in Sheol; we remain,
A man who had two sons.
No question which the favoured!

I could be Cain to his Abel.

* *Psalm 35: 14*

Survivors

We have seen them go, the elders.
First, the survivors
Of the war to end all wars (which did not).
I recall my father
Sitting upright in bed, hair wild,
Eyes fixed on some remembered horror,
Furiously conducting
An invisible orchestra.

And I recall
At Oxford, a gentle poet
Quivering from head to foot
As he lectured on the Romantics.
I remember also
The young Auden, plum in mouth;
Spender's aureole of bright hair;
Menuhin pale, fur-hatted,
As we waited after the concert.

Down, down they go, the elders,
Those who helped to form us:
Tolkien, Lewis, Helen Gardner,
Charles Williams, David Cecil:
Is it we, now who are the survivors?

Our children, busy with the business of living,
Remember birthdays, send gifts at Christmas,
Visit from time to time;
Regard us courteously, kindly,
Making allowance
For our stiff joints, our odd habits,
Outmoded beliefs.
The grandchildren
Glance up from their computers,
And wonder how much longer.

Lying awake, as the heart
Judders, halts, recovers,
Ah, so do we.

PLACES

West Wittering

In a windless hollow
My Child lies sleeping,
Secure from sorrow
And the searching wind.

O sleep! rest while you may
Free from harm.
The wind will search you out
To alarm.

Slumber and peace depart
Your waking eyes.
Death, to the pure heart,
Grants Paradise.

Runswick

Waters, cease your restless striving,
Ceaselessly, senselessly driving
On the salt strand of the sterile shore.
For the sand is infertile;
Prolific only in shells and the curiously fronded seaweed,
Food neither for man nor beast.

Lover, cease your restless urging,
Salt tides of love, your surging
Through the narrow channels of my barren being.
For I am unfruitful;
Prolific only in dreams and the linking of words in verses,
Good neither for man nor child.

#

In New York, city of skyscrapers,
One lives in an apartment
The symbol for which is this:

#

Regard the symbol: the pattern is significant.
One has (it is seen) a certain spatial position –
Four walls, a floor and a ceiling –
Defined by number and letter
From the pressure of countless others
Above, both sides, and below,
Whom one rarely sees, hears with a vague resentment,
And never wishes to know.
Number and letter are important;
They distinguish the individual.
Mail addressed to a skyscraper
May not get delivered.

When the rain at night rattles the blinded windows
I consider my position,
Suspended (contrary to gravity)
In a brick box somewhere above Manhattan;
Kept without roots or roof
In an artificial air
Adjusted by unseen hands.
Can this be what God intended?

The rain descends
(O doux bruit de la pluie,
Par terre et sur les toits!)
Soft rain in Sussex, torrents on Nakasero,
But here, in my apartment,
Merely a darkening of grimy windows.
No roof overhead for the feet of the rain to dance on,
No garden below for the scent of the rain to sweeten.
Cut off, shut in, I stay in my apartness.

O withered is the garland of my heart.

MOODS

Seagulls

The hours of silence are precious to me,
When through the window I see the gulls wheeling
Against the expressionless sky, as blank as Time;
And I can lie in release, not feeling
My personal griefs, my private ills;
Being diffused in the flight of a bird.

East Wind

Nothing to call me out,
No-one to keep me in.
Not the seagull-shrieking children
Nor the moans of the old house,
As its digestion settles.
Even the phone is Ansa-ed,
And the post pocketed.
I am alone with myself,
And this paper and pen.
Thank God! now I begin.

Waiting for Blood

It's a rum go,
Waiting for blood.
Every woman
Ever born,
Maiden, mistress, mother,
(Even Mary, ever-Virgin?
O, most especially she!)
Has stood, as I do now,
Peering, testing, pondering,
In hope, relief, or terror
(What shall I do? O where can I go?)
Waiting for blood.

No man
Has ever shared this vigil.
(They can't understand.)
One quick fling
And it's over, for them.
But for us
The ache in the belly,
The hope, the fear,
Delight,
Dismay,
Waiting for blood.

For some, of course,
It's a life-sentence,
Nine months in advance.

It's a rum go.

PRAYER

Early Waking

Time
To winnow the harvest of dreams,
To unravel the chorus of birds;
Time
To uncoil, yawn, stretch,
To re-inhabit the body,
Salute
The stiff hip, the bruised toe
(Old comrade; new acquaintance).
Time
To breathe deep;
To become aware
Of self,
Of You,
Quietly there.
Time to give thanks;
Time
To be.

Quietude

O, the blessedness of silence!
Time without times,
Without the watch of clocks,
The chatter and whine of radio,
The flashiness of the telly!
Time to become still,
Restless fingers relaxed,
Breathing quiet,
Spirit at peace;
The person personal,
Not diffused, not scattered hither and thither,
Becoming aware
Of self,
Of You,
Still there;
Still
And here.

Deo Gratias.

Prayer
in time of Frost

Fasten me
To You;
I cannot hold.
Let me not slip
Into the cold;
Not drop, dear Lord,
Not fall,
Into the cold.

Shrift

Coming again to grace,
After long absence, I recall the way,
The winding stair,
The silence and the peace;
And You are there.

Heart pounding, mind in spate,
I kneel, and I am blessed.
My listed sins become irrelevant.
Words falter, but the intent
Is honoured: ah, my Lord!
You do the rest.

KALENDAR

*Ballad for Epiphany**

Three Kings came riding out of the East,
Noble each rider, weary each beast;
But they were riding as to a feast!
                    Little One, we are coming.

Caspar's locks were golden and free,
His skin was fair for all to see.
He rode a horse of pedigree:
                    Jesu, we are coming.

Melchior's skin was yellow as milk,
His hair a fall of jet-black silk.
A mule he rode, of Eastern ilk:
                    Master, we are coming.

Balthasar's skin was black as night,
Black his hair, and curling tight,
But he looked a king, and he sat upright,
For Balthasar rode a camel!
                    Saviour, we are coming.

* *January 6th*

*St. Valentine**

On the flower-stalls, red roses
Stand stiff, up to their ankles in water,
Tall, innocent of thorns or scent.
"Lovely blooms, sir, five quid a throw"
And are swiftly wrapped.

Within doors
In the scented warmth
We're talking serious money.
A heart of gold
Gleams, in a satin casket.
Voices are reverent,
Credit cards flash.

High in the peartree
A blackbird hunches
Ruffled in the twilight,
As a half moon hesitates above.
His eye, for once
Not on the next worm,
He's spying for a mate.

The mild-eyed saint
Hears, far-off, Ophelia's song,
And wonders why.

** Feast Day February 14th*

Annunciation*

The B.V.M.
Was
Not
A woman priest
Nor
A deaconess;
Not
A lay reader
Nor
A parish worker;
And certainly not a nun!

But
She said
YES!
And God thought
She would do.

How about you?

* *Feast Day March 25th*

*St. Mark**

I like
Your brief Gospel
Where everything happens
"Immediately",
As if the Lord
Was in a tearing hurry.
(Well, He only had three years,
And so much to do.)

You were the first
Of the Gospel-makers,
Giving us the bones of the story,
The heart of the matter.

Matthew the Jew, Luke the Physician, mystic John
All followed in your footsteps,
Adding their own flavours
To your basic stock.

Brave Mark!
It takes courage
To be a fore-runner;
Which is why your emblem
Is, properly,
The Lion.

** Feast Day April 25th*

*St. Philip & St. James**

Philip and James,
Pip and Jim,
Come in with a slightly
Doubtful grin,
For they know very well
What the lasses and lads
Of Padstow – of Cornwall –
Of all Merrie England
Have been up to, this night,
To bring in the May,
Among the leaves so green-o.

Good Mother Church
Like a spring-cleaning wife,
Sets about blessing
The healing wells
And the magic stones
In the hollow hills.

But the Green Man peers,
Though carven in stone,
From farmyards, from gardens,
Aye, even from churches!
While the ’Obby ’Oss prances
Rears and advances
As Padstow dances
To bring in the May,
Among the leaves so green-o.

Philip and James,
Pip and Jim,
Get no more than
A meaningful grin,
And a word in the ear
As the dancers draw near:
To keep up old customs
’Tis surely no sin?
And to bring in the May,
Among the leaves so green-o.

* *Feast Day May 1st*

*St. Peter**

Dear Peter,
What a comfort you are!
Sometimes Christianity
Seems too good, too pure and holy
For people like me,
Full of faults and failings.
(Oh, I know them so well,
And keep on doing them
In spite of repentance!)

You, dear muddle-head,
Full of good intentions,
Jumped into situations
Feet first;
Babbling nonsense
Up there on the mountain;
Rejecting the Lord
At that Maundy supper,
Then suddenly wanting
Total immersion!
In the end,
It took the crow of a cock
To bring you to your senses.

Even your death
(Horrible, shameful)
Had a slight touch
Of the ridiculous:
Upside-down,
A parody of your Master's.

Yet you, Peter, are the Rock
Eternal, beneath our feet.
You hold the Keys of the Kingdom.
Forgiven sinners
Look up; stretch out a hand
which you take.

** Feast Day June 29th*

*St. Mary Magdalen**

Faithful? Yes, indeed.
But no word spoken –
Neither at supper,
Nor at the foot of the Cross –
Nothing but tears;
Till, in that dewy morning,
"Rabboni!"
Said it all.

** Feast Day July 22nd*

*Transfiguration**

On this day
A new chasm opened
As the atom shattered
In a mushroom cloud;
And men shuddered
In awful fear.

On this day
A new vision opened
As You appeared
In a cloud of glory;
And the three trembled
With awe-full fear.

Perhaps we, also,
Need to go away
To a lonely place
(With Peter, James, and Joanna)
To see You, Lord,
In terror and glory,
On this Day?

** Feast Day August 6th*

Michaelmas*

Michael, Archangel
Clad in shining armour,
Greatest of the four
(Gabriel, Raphael,
Uriel your brethren),
In the cosmic battle
You toppled Lucifer
From his place in Heaven,
Down to reign in Hades
And prowl about this Earth.

With such a c.v., Sir,
It's really most surprising
That your emblem down here
Should be so very modest.
A sunflower? a peony?
Something big and splashy?
Nothing of the sort, ye hosts!
– A little purple daisy.

** Feast Day September 29th*

Litany for St. Luke*

Sit by the fire time,
Darkening at tea time,
Letters to friends time,
Brooding with books time;
Poems emerging.

Beeches ablaze time,
Fall of the leaf time,
Bonfire-y smell time,
Mushrooms to pick time;
Poems ripe.

* *Feast Day October 18th*

*St. Andrew**

How was it for you, Andrew,
Always second fiddle
To that flamboyant brother
Simon Peter?
Did you sigh, privately,
When he put his foot in it
AGAIN?
Your mother said
"He's the quiet one: a good lad.
Follows his brother like a dog."

But you, Andrew, are the one
Who stands at the gate of the year,
Janus, the two-headed,
Looking before and after.
Behind you
The long long Sundays of Trinity;
And ahead
Advent,
The coming of the New.
Stand firm, Andrew,
Beacon the dark!

** Feast Day November 30th*

*St. Nicolas**

Patron of sailors, protector of children,
What an excellent fellow you are, St. Nick!
You shine like a star
In the dark of December;
Like the stars that came out
While the sailors slept
After the storm,
In Benjamin Britten's *Cantata*.
I love his tale
Of the pickled boys
Miraculously restored
To their weeping mothers;
And the gifts, tossed secretly
In at a window,
Which entitled you "Father Christmas".
Where would we be without you,
O good and generous saint?

If I were young and hearty
I'd make a pilgrimage
To your birthplace at Myra,
And give thanks on the spot.
As it is, I say *(con brio)*
Bless you, St. Nick!

* *Feast Day December 6th*

Cat-er-waul

Villain!
Accursed, smooth and smiling villain!
Perched so nonchalantly
On the wall (*my* wall, incidentally)
Whiskers unruffled,
Your elegant black-and-white
Sleek and shining
As any highclass waiter
(And as insolent)
Your yellow eyes
Bland as butter;
While below, in the flowerbed,
Havoc is cried!
Primroses and pansies
Uprooted,
Daffodils demolished,
Soil scattered,
And, in the midst,
Your triumphant token
Stinks in the sun.
(Why the deuce don't you cover it up
Like a *proper* cat?)

I have tried *Go-Cat*:
You did not go.
Also *Scent-Off*
Which failed to send you off.
What next? I have seen
In Garden Centres
A plastic cat,
A black cat with enormous eyes
Shining, day and night.
Does it work?

Our ancient Tigger,
As usual, asleep
On my bed, in a heap,
No longer rouses
To defend his territory.
Shall I stoop to feigning
With a plastic cat?
O Isis, O Osiris,
Tell me that!

Thoughts on being asked to write a poem about the Millennium

Is it really TWO thousand ages,
Dear Lord,
Since you first turned up,
A squalling baby
In a cattle shed,
A lad in a carpenter's shop,
A vagrant with a band of – well,
Not very reputable friends?

It didn't work, did it, lord?
People still go on
Hating one another,
Taking it out on the other chap,
Because he's the wrong colour,
Or race, or religion, whatever.
Is it time to try again?
Come in a posh suit,
With a big car,
And a pocketful of dollars?
Would anybody care?

I think the baby
Would have a better chance:
At least, His mother would listen.

EPILOGUE

Wordsmith

Hostages to fortune
These words,
New born from the womb of the spirit.

Do I dare
Send you forth
To baptism
In the cold font?
To stand
Stiffly in line,
Like a child
In his first school clothes?

Other eyes will see,
Others hear,
And judge.
Love is shown in the letting go.
Go with God, little words.

COMING FORTH
Poems Previously Unpublished

Internet

Homeless words
Traverse the ether,
Storm-tossed birds
Seeking shelter,
And cluster under my roof.

Uninvited
Your presence compels
Attention;
Your existence
Requires a response
I am reluctant to give.

Do I neglect you at my peril,
Trivia from outer space?

December 1998

Interlude On A Journey

In Ipplepen, on Monday night
suddenly hearing in the distance the sound of a crow
and being transported, instantaneously
twenty-three years, to the West of Ireland, to
timeless… ageless… wind-blown, green, rocky,
harsh, soft land… the land itself crying out.
Other flashbacks: to the hills and the dales
of England, evoked
unexpectedly
by narrow lanes, wooded riverbanks and valleys
and by nettles in the hedge. Unexpectedly
taken to a place of simplicity,
deep sorrow, solid work, persistence,
and age… – age that cries out for
respect, value, and all the things
which young England today has no time for.

By majority, young England is in a hurry
to reach the twenty-first Century;
young England is urgent
to lose its past; young England today is
impatient with itself and with seriousness
and with the idea of weighty matters. And yet
the light in their eyes can still be seen –
it can still fire, like a cannon from
one of Raleigh's ships. In those eyes
one's eyes are caught, and in those sights
one cannot be lost.

A.

How I should miss you,
Infuriating man!
Familiar as an old sock
(And as smelly?)
A thick and comforting
Layer of protection
Against whatsoever
Slings and arrows
Daily living might turn up.
(A stone in a shoe,
A thorn in a foot,
A chilblain on a toe.)
And, like an old sock,
Taken (shamefully) for granted
Until life's wear and tear
Made itself felt
And the harshness of real life
Began to get through to me.
O, how I miss
Your sometimes clumsy
And loving (so, loving) comfort!

July 20th

Contract

We must give back to God
The south zone of ourself -
The soles of our feet -
Into His keeping; east, and west,
Our sides are already contracted.
There remains our north,
The busy brain,
Forever sending and receiving,
Though all its messages now scrambled.
Grant it quietus.

And the heart? the centre of the web?
Ah, that is His already.

February 2nd 2000

To Be A Pilgrim

What hinders?
Late nights,
Stale air,
Much conversation;
Envious thoughts,
Wasted time,
Jealous fears:
Sins unrepented.

And helps?
Quiet sleep,
Auspicious dreams,
Hopeful waking;
Wrongs discarded,
Kindnesses remembered,
And (Herbert's best)
A heart's thanksgiving.

February 12th 2000

In Memoriam
R. S. T.

The death of an old poet
Is the withering of the last leaf
On a shrivelled bough;
Ah, but the blossom
Is radiant, immortal
On the shriven stem.

for September 25th 2000

Preservation

Preserved? perhaps.
But not as flies in amber,
Fossilised
To grace a woman's throat;
Or butterflies,
Their fluttering fixed and finished,
Impaled on pins
In someone's prized collection.

Rather as ginger
In your marmalade,
Adding a frisson
To breakfast toast?
Or Shelley's roseleaves
When the rose is dead?
Kept, anyway, for a purpose
Which it is now our lifeswork
To discover.

December 2000

On Being 80

It's not just the shock
Of seeing one's friends
Drop off the twig
(Especially if younger than oneself!)
It's the nasty surprise
Of the little things
One can no longer do
(Or only with enormous difficulty)
Such as getting OUT of the bath;
Or cutting toenails;
Or wearing size 16!
It's getting breathless on stairs;
And being called 'Dear'
By people in shops;
And – shame of shames –
Needing a stick
To cross the road;
It's losing one's memory
For the little things
One did ten minutes ago –
That IS the end!

June 22 2001

Christmas 2001

You came with no requests,
Only a cry;
And Mary's breasts
Filled with milk
In reply.

Faint, down the years,
We hear that cry.
Our meagre love
On near and dear is spent;
Love the unlovable
Was what You meant.

2001

Joy's View

A summer's day, a hard bright heat
A brimming church, a long brown box
My hand squeezed in comfort
as father and son speak of the spirit.
Out of nowhere, a tidal wave
breaks inside my eyes, my heart.
Two by two we step out slow
Arms lay her down to rest
The husband drops a rose
with earth, the sister's soft farewell.
A surge of pain, the salt sting clears
we lift up our eyes to the hills
A family united in grief and love
and Joy's view.

DF 8.6.07
(hoping Mum would approve this pale imitation)

Joy French

1921 - 2007

ISBN 978-1-7385743-1-5

www.ingramcontent.com/pod-product-compliance
Lightning Source LLC
LaVergne TN
LVHW012112160826
845678LV00014B/3050

* 9 7 8 1 7 3 8 5 7 4 3 1 5 *